SRI LANKA

Dan Colwell

D1796098

J·P·M
PUBLICATIONS

Contents

This Way Sri Lanka   3

Flashback   7

On the Scene   13

   Colombo   13

     Fort 14, The Pettah 15, Galle Face Green 16, Cinnamon Gardens 16, Around Colombo 18

   Southwest and South Coast   21

     Negombo 21, Kalutara 22, Beruwala and Bentota 22, Ambalangoda 23, Hikkaduwa 23, Galle 24, Unawatuna 26, Weligama 26, Matara 26, Tangalla 27, Hambantota 27, Yala National Park 27

   Kandy and the Hill Country   29

     Kandy 29, Nuwara Eliya 33, Around the Hill Country 34

   Ancient Cities   37

     Anuradhapura 37, Mihintale 41, Aukana 41, Polonnaruwa 41, Sigiriya 46, Dambulla 47

   East Coast   48

     Trincomalee 48

Cultural Notes   50

Shopping   52

Dining Out   54

Sports   56

The Hard Facts   57

Index   64

Fold-out maps

   Sri Lanka
   Colombo, Kandy, Anuradhapura

This Way Sri Lanka

Resplendent Land

At first sight Sri Lanka is a thousand shades of green, from the concentrated emerald of the coconut palms and the deep jungle to the luminous hues of innumerable tea bushes and the tender pallor of young rice. But on closer inspection this small island nation reveals a much richer variety of colours, scenery, culture and people.

Ringed by sweeping golden-sand beaches and sparkling blue seas, the island also boasts forests roamed by elephants, level plains encrusted with 1,000-m-high (3,280-ft) rocks, and highlands at its heart. Here you're suddenly confronted with a very different world of pine trees, trout farms and cool evening air. The highest point is Mt Pidurutalagala at 2,524 m (8,281 ft), but the most revered is Adam's Peak. Sacred to Buddhists, Hindus and Muslims alike, it's ascended by pilgrims en masse each December.

Sri Lanka's natural wonders are complemented by man-made masterpieces stretching back more than 2,000 years. Massive-domed gleaming white shrines, great palaces and vast irrigation tanks can be found among the ancient ruins of Anuradhapura and Polonnaruwa; medieval rock temples, botanical gardens and national parks, 17th-century Dutch forts and grand British colonial mansions and hotels abound throughout the country.

Perhaps the most amazing thing of all is that these sights are so close to each other; you can get from cosmopolitan Colombo to tranquil beaches, lush jungles, ancient cities and mountainous tea country in just a few hours.

No one has recognized the wonder of this beautiful country more than its inhabitants have. When they changed the name from Ceylon in 1972, they honoured it by adding the title "Sri" —meaning "resplendent" or "favoured by fortune"—to the old pre-colonial name of Lanka.

Rich Resources

Sitting at the centre of the ancient east-west trade route, Sri Lanka has always been widely famed for its richly exotic natural resources, and was known even to the Greeks and Romans. Arabian traders reached the island in the 8th century, hungry for its spices. Their name for it, Serendib, gave rise to the word "serendipity", the gift of discovering valuable or pleasant things by accident.

It was the island's great quantities of cinnamon—easily collected, and sold in Europe at a high price—that lured the Portuguese and later the Dutch here. Modern taste buds, however, are more likely to be tantalized by the truly exotic range of fruit that the tropical climate produces, from the juiciest mangoes and papaya to the rare flavours and aromas of the rambutan, durian and mangosteen.

But probably the greatest natural resource—certainly the best-loved—is one that has served as bulldozer, crane, and heavy-goods vehicle from the time the great temples and palaces were built at Anuradhapura over 2,000 years ago: the elephant. Hundreds are still used on building sites and in timber haulage, and you'll see them wherever you go, working in villages in the jungle and in downtown Colombo, leading the processions at festival time or cooling off in rivers. They are best viewed in their natural habitat. Some 2,000 beasts roam wild, mostly in nature reserves like Yala and Wilpattu, where herds of up to 80 elephants provide an unforgettably majestic sight.

Their central importance in Sri Lankan life is attested to by the elephant carvings that adorn temples and other public buildings both ancient and modern, and, however less exalted, in the pervasive presence of elephant memorabilia among souvenirs.

An Intriguing People

Almost 19 million people occupy the island's 65,610 sq km (25,332 sq miles), an area slightly smaller than Ireland. They are notably well-educated, with a literacy rate of more than 90%, and while not rich—the average income is under US$20 per week—show few signs of the grinding poverty seen among their near neighbours on the subcontinent.

Without doubt, modern Sri Lankans constitute an intriguing mix of cultures, reflecting the country's tumultuous history. There are four main ethnic groups; the predominantly Buddhist Sinhalese, who make up almost three-quarters of the population; Hindu Tamils of south

1 **THE BEST GROUP OF FRESCOES** Halfway up the famous rock fortress at **Sigiriya** are 21 marvellous wall paintings depicting beautiful, wide-eyed "celestial maidens". Dating back 1,500 years, they inspired male contemporaries to graffiti passionate comments on a nearby wall.

Around 70 per cent of Sri Lanka's population follows the Buddhist creed.

Indian origin, many of whom were brought here by the British to work on tea plantations in the 19th century, and who are about 18% of the total; smaller groups of Muslims, descended from medieval traders; and Burghers, whose lighter skins and European names derive from 16th- and 17th-century colonization.

Sadly, it's often a combustible mix as well. A population which is uniformly friendly and considerate to visitors has at times wrought terrible violence upon itself. In the ongoing conflict, which started in the early 1980s, Tamil separatists have countered what they see as discrimination against their community by waging war against the dominant Sinhalese. An end to the conflict has appeared in sight many times. But the problem of how to reconcile the demands of the Tamils with the desire of the government to hold the country together and satisfy the Sinhalese majority has proved intractable.

Today, much of the island is as beautifully idyllic and safe for tourists as ever. But until a solution to the troubles is found, the main Tamil parts of the island—including the renowned beaches of the north and east coasts—remain virtually out of bounds for tourists.

Flashback

Early Inhabitants

The first settlers were the Veddahs, tribes of hunter-gatherers who were part of the same ethnic group as the hill tribes of south India. Their possession of Sri Lanka came to an end in the 5th century BC through invasion from the mainland. According to early chronicles written by Buddhist monks, known as the *Mahavamsa*, the island was conquered by Prince Vijaya and 700 followers from northern India, who found the place inhabited by demons. Vijaya destroyed them and went on to establish a great dynasty.

In fact, the takeover was a more drawn-out process. Merchants from India had long traded with the island. When colonization from India began in earnest, it's probable that most of the native Veddahs were gradually absorbed by the newcomers. Indeed, it's thought that a distinct Sinhalese language and culture developed out of this synthesis.

From the 3rd century BC, Tamils from southern India began migrating to the east coast.

Anuradhapura Period

In the centuries after the conquest, several different Sinhalese kingdoms rose and fell. The strongest and most magnificent developed at Anuradhapura in the island's northern plains. In the mid-3rd century BC, a mission led by Mahinda, son of Ashoka, the great Buddhist emperor of India, converted the Anuradhapuran king Devanampiya Tissa (reigned 250–221 BC) to Buddhism. With the subsequent extension of the kingdom's power throughout Sri Lanka, Buddhism became the accepted religion of all the Sinhalese.

Buddhism proved a remarkably energizing force in Anuradhapuran society, and the unified culture it produced created considerable political and economic strength. Powerful kings such as Tissa, Dutugemenu (161–137 BC) and Mahasena (AD 276–303) built huge temples, monasteries and great palaces, as well as vast reservoirs to irrigate the rice fields.

Anuradhapura remained the island's principal city for almost 1,400 years despite suffering many invasions by south Indian Hindu kingdoms. Possibly even more of a strain on resources were the retaliatory raids by the Sinhalese on the mainland. By the 10th century, the kingdom found itself increasingly drawn into dangerous south Indian regional battles, something that ultimately proved its undoing. In 993, an alliance with the Pandyan kingdom led to it being invaded by their enemies, the Colas, an event that put an end to the Anuradhapura era.

Polonnaruwa Period

It wasn't until 1070 that the Sinhalese, under King Vijayabahu, were able to regain control of the country. The king decided to abandon the old capital and build an entirely new one 75 km (47 miles) southeast at Polonnaruwa, which was further away from the Indian mainland and easier to defend. Sinhalese art and culture reached new heights under King Parakramabahu I (1153–86) and his successor, Nissankamalla (1187–96). But by the 13th century, the kingdom was fragmenting under ineffective rulers and renewed external threats. After 1214, power fell into the hands of mainly south Indian factions and the Sinhalese gradually shifted southwards, setting up a series of different capitals at Dambadeniya, Kurunegala and Gampola.

By the 15th century, the political map had changed dramatically. In the wake of Sinhalese withdrawal from the north, a Tamil kingdom had been established, centred on the Jaffna Peninsula. The main Sinhalese kingdom had finally set up its capital in Kotte, near present-day Colombo. Meanwhile, a second, smaller Sinhalese kingdom was tucked away behind its mountain defences at Kandy. Divided and weakened, the island was ripe for further foreign conquest.

The Portuguese Arrive

By the turn of the 16th century, the most dynamic power in the Indian Ocean was Portugal. In 1505, a Portuguese fleet under Lourenço de Almeida was blown by strong winds into Colombo. Almeida received a friendly welcome from the king of Kotte and quickly saw the commercial and strategic potential of the island. Within 13 years, the Portuguese had won concessions on the lu-

2 **THE TWO BEST STATUES OF THE BUDDHA** Sri Lanka contains countless images of the Buddha. But the two most exquisite are the wonderfully expressive standing Buddha carved from granite at **Gal Vihara** in Polonnaruwa; and the huge statue at **Aukana**, 13 m (43 ft) high, whose face is illuminated each morning by the first rays of the sun.

crative spice and cinnamon trade and had permission to build a fort at Colombo.

The rest of the century witnessed concerted Portuguese efforts to take possession of the island. In this they were helped by further Sri Lankan disunity. The kingdom of Kotte split into three warring states in 1521 and proved unable to resist increasing Portuguese influence. By 1597, the Portuguese took formal control of Kotte, followed in 1619 by the annexation of Jaffna. Try as they might, they never managed to defeat Kandy, which remained an independent kingdom despite several expeditions launched against it.

The Portuguese were harsh rulers and zealous Catholics. Buddhist and Hindu temples were destroyed and intense missionary activity attempted to convert the population, although only the upper-class Sinhalese, keen to keep in with their masters, complied. In the face of such provocation, the kingdom of Kandy felt it had little choice but to seek assistance from a new European power in the region.

The Dutch Take Over

The first Dutch contact with Kandy was in 1602, when Joris van Spilbergen met with King Vimala Dharma Surya and offered military support. It soon became apparent that the Dutch merely wanted to replace the Portuguese as the dominant colonial power. They were particularly keen on Sri Lanka's cinnamon, and after their fleet had captured Batticaloa on the east coast in 1638, they were granted a cinnamon trade monopoly by King Vimala's successor, Rajasinha II.

During this time, the Kandyans launched separate attacks on Portuguese coastal towns, but without a navy were unable to claim a decisive victory. Meanwhile, the Dutch acted in their own interests, signing peace treaties with Portugal, then taking up arms against them when it was expedient. However, Portuguese power was on the wane. The Dutch chased them out of Colombo in 1656 after a long siege, and finally expelled them from Jaffna two years later, when all former Portuguese possessions were in their hands. The Kandyans, too, were shut out by the Dutch, and they retreated to their mountain stronghold.

The Dutch established administrative centres in Galle, Colombo and Jaffna, and settled down to reap huge profits from the spice trade. There was an attempt to convert people to the Dutch Reformed Church and Catholicism was made illegal, but again Buddhism proved too strong a force to subvert.

As the century came to a close, upheaval in Europe once more had profound effects on Sri Lanka. The Netherlands' gradual decline was sealed with the wars of the French Revolution, when the French army invaded Holland. The British, by now in control in eastern India and at war with France, moved in on Sri Lanka, where the Dutch surrendered to them in 1796.

British Rule

The British initially saw Sri Lanka as a temporary acquisition and ruled it from Madras. Its strategic position in relation to the Raj soon proved so useful that Ceylon, the British name for the island, was made a crown colony in 1802. As they set about organizing trade and government, the British administration soon realised the danger in allowing an independent native kingdom to dominate the highlands. Making clever use of internal disputes between the king and his chiefs, the British managed to conquer Kandy in 1815, creating the first unified state on the island in several centuries.

The British wrought many changes on the face of Sri Lanka, not least the development of vast tea, rubber and coconut plantations. They also brought in thousands of Tamils from southern India to work as labourers. Later in the century, the port of Colombo was developed into the country's most important commercial centre, and English became the official language of government and education.

This last development particularly rankled, and in reaction both Buddhist and Hindu schools were established. Opposition to colonial rule from a more politically conscious class of Sri Lankans grew. The British riposted with constitutional reforms in the early 20th century, but these only gave "educated" Sri Lankans the vote. A more militant nationalism erupted with civil disturbances in 1915, and concessions made to nationalists only increased their demands for political power.

During World War II, the island played an important strategic role in the conflict with Japan, serving as Allied Headquarters in 1943–44. With the break-up of the British Raj immediately after the war, Ceylon was granted dominion status, followed by full independence early in 1948.

Modern Sri Lanka

The British legacy to Sri Lanka was a system of parliamentary democracy that has managed to survive subsequent economic crises and civil war. The first governments were headed by the United National Party (UNP) under English-educated leaders, who were conservative in style and buoyed up by a flourishing trade in tea and rubber. However, the mid-1950s saw a downturn in the economy and the formation of Sinhalese nationalist parties such as the Sri Lanka Freedom Party (SLFP), founded by the charismatic Solomon Bandaranaike. Committed to making Sinhalese the national language, giving state support to Buddhism and promoting a form of socialism, the SLFP won power, but inevitably alienated the Tamils. The dangerous forces unleashed at this time led to the assassination of Bandaranaike by a Buddhist monk in 1959.

His wife, Sirimavo, led the party in the 1960s and pushed through its policies on both language and the state's role in the economy. In 1972, the country's name was officially changed from Ceylon to Sri Lanka and a new constitution was written, creating the role of president as head of state. Power alternated with the UNP through the next two decades, but the economy worsened further, leading to the abandonment of socialist policies. The result of dissatisfaction with the Colombo government was the rise of more extreme groups among both Sinhalese and Tamils. In the early 1980s the Liberation Tigers of Tamil Eelam (LTTE) commenced a bloody separatist war in the north and east of the country, while anti-Tamil riots in 1983 saw mobs attack Tamils and their property in Colombo, Nuwara Eliya and elsewhere.

The job of government had become one of how to keep the country together, and the two methods employed alternated between pursuing war and seeking peace. In 1987, the UNP government of JR Jayawardene offered the Tamils an autonomous northeast province within Sri Lanka, to be monitored by Indian peace-keeping troops. Three years later his successor, Ranasinghe Premadasa, negotiated the withdrawal of the Indian force and renewed the military campaign against the LTTE. He was assassinated by a suicide bomber, suspected of being a member of the LTTE, in 1993.

Recent years have seen increased hopes for a peace settlement. The People's Alliance Party, a coalition of the SLFP and other groups, came to power in 1994 under Chandrika Kumaratunga, daughter of Solomon Bandaranaike, and her government has been in talks with the LTTE. Much of the country is unaffected by the troubles. But until the hostilities end, it seems unlikely that this "resplendent" nation can fully realise its economic and cultural potential.

On the Scene

The first port of call for most visitors is the city of Colombo, with its museums, monuments and great Pettah bazaar. Colombo is also the nation's transport hub. Sri Lanka is small enough for you to get to any of the nation's main tourist spots from there in a day, even at the leisurely pace its roads and railways dictate. It's just a short hop to the wonderful golden beaches of the southwest coast. Trains and buses from Colombo head to the cool climes of the Hill Country, with its spectacular scenery and vast tea plantations; to the ancient capital at Kandy, home to the most important religious site in Sri Lanka; and to the magnificent ruins at Anuradhapura and Polonnaruwa in the northern plains, thousand-year-old centres of Sinhalese culture.

COLOMBO
Fort, The Pettah, Galle Face Green, Cinnamon Gardens, Around Colombo

Sri Lanka's largest city is also one of the biggest ports in the Indian Ocean and the gateway through which most of the country's foreign trade passes. It has been serving maritime commerce since at least the 5th century AD, when it was visited by the Chinese traveller Fa-hsien. Arab traders settled here during the 8th century, and the port was used by both the Portuguese and the

Dutch, although it ranked second in importance to Galle. Colombo came into its own during the British era when, following the conquest of Kandy and the opening of the Suez Canal, political and commercial interests shifted northwards, and it became the country's main port and capital.

With a population approaching 700,000, Colombo is a teeming, modern south Asian business city, whose tropical steaminess is alleviated by ocean breezes. Five-star hotels and restaurants and a thriving shopping area rub shoul-

Candy-striped Jami-ul-Alfar is the most striking of the city's mosques.

ders with some fine colonial architecture. To cap it all, the beautiful beaches of the southwest coast are within easy reach.

Fort

As its name suggests, the heart of colonial Colombo began life as a fortress, built by the Portuguese on land granted by the king of Kotte in the early 16th century. It was later reinforced by the Dutch, though little of that era remains and many of the grand buildings along its wide streets date from the Victorian period. With many of Sri Lanka's biggest hotels and highrises, shops, banks and company headquarters packed in, the area retains its historic importance in Sri Lankan life.

Clock Tower

A trusty Fort landmark since it was erected in 1857, the Clock Tower, located at the junction of Chatham Street and Janadhipathi Mawatha (formerly Queen's Street), makes a good place to start a tour of the area. If it resembles a lighthouse, that's because it also doubled as one until the 1950s.

President's House

Directly north of the Clock Tower, heavy police security tells you you're near the Sri Lankan president's residence, Janadhipathi Medura. It has long been a centre of power. The elegant, whitewashed mansion dates from the time of the last Dutch governor at the end of the 18th century. Under the British governors who followed, it became known as Queen's House.

Across Janadhipathi Mawatha, the imposing, gleaming white General Post Office seems just as powerful a symbol of British imperial rule. North of the President's House, Gordon Gardens contain a statue of Queen Victoria and a stone engraved by the early Portuguese colonists. For the time being, however, access is severely restricted for security reasons.

York Street

Follow Janadhipathi Mawatha round to the right to busy York Street. Fort's main shopping thoroughfare is famous for its venerable 19th-century commercial buildings, most notably the red-fronted and resolutely old-fashioned Miller's and Cargill's department stores. At the harbour end, take a break at the Grand Oriental Hotel. It's a fine colonial-era watering hole that was once the first stop for travellers rolling off the passenger ships from Europe. The fourth-floor Harbour Room restaurant is well worth a visit if only for what is undoubtedly the best view of Colombo's vast, bustling port.

St Peter's Church

A short distance from the hotel, the Anglican church originally had a more secular function as part of the Dutch governor's banqueting hall. It was first used as a place of worship in 1804, later becoming the British garrison church. Inside, the walls are covered with memorials to the regiments and colonial agents who served here.

Buddha Jayanthi Dagoba

The shrine is located on Marine Drive and looks like a cross between traditional Buddhist architecture and the Space Shuttle. Built in the 1950s to celebrate the Buddha's 2,500th birthday, it was perched on top of concrete stilts so as to catch the eye of those arriving by sea.

The Pettah

Just inland from Fort, the Pettah is a full-blooded south Asian bazaar that bursts out from the grid street-plan. The Dutch called it the Oude Stad ("Old Town"), as it was a Portuguese residential area long before they moved in. During British rule it acquired its current name, which derives from the Tamil word *pettai*, meaning "outside the fort".

Bazaar

The Pettah bazaar is one of Sri Lanka's great experiences, and best enjoyed by simply hurling yourself into the tumult of people, noise, colours, smells, and cries from shopkeepers eager for your custom. You'll find everything under the sun on sale—clothes and cloth, fruit and fish, watches, jewellery, silver and brassware, electrical goods, toys—but be prepared to take part in the favourite local sport of haggling.

Dutch Period Museum

From the midst of the hullaballoo rises the stout, colonnaded façade of this late-17th-century Dutch townhouse on Prince Street. It was the home of ex-governor Thomas van Rhee in the 1690s, and under the British was used variously as a military hospital, police training centre and post office. Recently restored, it now contains a very interesting museum with maps, models, furniture, paintings and panels exploring the many facets of Dutch colonial society in Sri Lanka.

Jami-ul-Alfar Mosque

Turn left onto Second Cross Street, where you'll find it hard to miss this extraordinary red-and-white-striped mosque, dating from 1909.

Wolfendahl Church

To the east of the mosque, Colombo's oldest church was built in 1749, and stands on the site of an earlier Portuguese church. Its gabled façade and unornamented interior are typical of the Dutch Reformed Church style. Be sure to take a look at the floors paved with fine old tombstones. Wolfendahl is a translation of the Portuguese name for the area, *Agoa de Luphe* meaning "dale of the wolves". As not a single wolf has ever set foot in Sri Lanka, it's probable that the first Portuguese settlers wrongly identified a pack of wild dogs.

Galle Face Green

This large, ocean-side expanse south of Fort was the brainchild of the governor, Sir Henry Ward, and completed in 1859. A contemporary marker stone tells that it was intended for use by the ladies and children of Colombo, and it's still hugely popular with the city's residents. As the sun goes down and the air cools, it becomes a lively playground packed with cricket players, kite flyers and food stalls, while joggers, walkers, family groups and courting couples make the most of the seafront promenade.

Presidential Secretariat

At the north end of the green, this impressive neoclassical building served as the nation's parliament until 1982. The bronze statues outside honour Sri Lanka's leading independence heroes.

Galle Face Hotel

The green's southern end boasts a superb relic of the colonial era. Dating from 1864, the hotel has a delightful verandah looking out over the ocean that's excellent for drinks at sundown.

MASKS

Mask-making is a living art, and the skills used by today's craftsmen have been handed down for generations. The masks are still used for dance and ceremonial purposes. They are made from *kaduru* wood (a type of balsa) that's been smoke-dried for a week, then hand-carved and painted in accordance with age-old precepts.

There are three types. *Raksha* masks are used in festivals and processions and most frequently seen featuring the *Naga*, or seven-headed cobra; *Kolam* masks come from the tradition of lowland village dramas and dance; *Sanni* masks are intended to ward off disease-bearing demons. These spectacular masks contain 18 faces representing the full range of afflictions which the demons might bring, from boils to bile. Placed in the right position in your house when you get home, it's a souvenir that might even keep the doctor away.

Cinnamon Gardens

The area southeast of Galle Face was once a huge cinnamon plantation. Now it's a famously exclusive residential district known by its post code, Colombo 7. The grand colonial-era mansions are inhabited by foreign diplomats and members of the Sri Lankan elite, and it's fascinating just to walk along such incongruously leafy, English-looking streets as Barnes Place or Horton Place. Afterwards, you can visit Colombo's best park and museum.

Vihara Maha Devi Park

Formerly called Victoria Park, this is a beautifully laid-out garden with lots of shady paths, lotus ponds and magnificent flowering trees. A delightful central avenue leads up to the imposing 1927 town hall which, with its neoclassical whitewashed portico and dome, resembles a scaled-down US Capitol.

National Museum

South of the park on Albert Crescent, the excellent Colombo National Museum was established in the 19th century and is housed in one of the country's most splendid colonial buildings. There are rooms dedicated to Sri Lanka's ancient cities, with some exquisite Buddhist and Hindu statues in bronze, stone and coral, a collection of superbly carved ivory combs and displays of weapons, painted vessels from the Kandyan era and old betel-nut pounders. The museum's range of traditional masks is first-rate, but perhaps nothing is as entertaining as the collection of presents to the President from foreign governments, which amounts to a perfect combination of the bizarre and the kitsch. The undoubted highlight, though, is the room given over to the regalia of Sri Vikrama Rajasinha, the last king of Kandy. Most of it was whisked off to England after the fall of Kandy in 1815, but given back in the 1930s by George V and Edward VIII. The crown, sword of state and throne, complete with lion armrests, are magnificent. Note that the museum is closed on Fridays and *poya* days.

Around Colombo

There are some enjoyable excursions to get you out of the city centre, none of which are more than 30 minutes from Fort by train or bus.

Dehiwala Zoo

Much of Sri Lanka's more interesting wildlife is notoriously shy of tourists, so this is probably the only way you'll see its big cats, reptiles and exotic birds. Set in splendid grounds 10 km (6 miles) south of Colombo, the zoo also has a wide range of animals from

The façade of Raja Maha Vihara temple is decorated with rows of chubby dwarves and elephants.

other tropical climes, an aquarium and afternoon performances by trained seals at 4 p.m. and elephants at 5.15 p.m.

Mount Lavinia

A few kilometres further south, Colombo's own resort is popular with everyone interested in escaping the city heat. There's a decent beach with plenty of low-key snack bars and, perched on a rocky promontory, the sumptuous Mount Lavinia Hotel. Dating from 1877, it was Governor Edward Barnes's personal beach hut until the British government balked at his lottery-winner's lifestyle and made him sell it.

Kelaniya Raja Maha Vihara

About 10 km (6 miles) east of Colombo, the pottery town of Kelaniya boasts one of Sri Lanka's most important temples, for the Buddha is believed to have preached at this site on the first of his three visits to the island. A dagoba was built on the spot, but was later the target for Tamil and Portuguese invaders. The temple has an acclaimed reclining Buddha and some fine 20th-century murals, one of them illustrating the legend of the Buddha's tooth kept in Kandy. Each January the temple is the centrepiece of a spectacular full moon festival that attracts thousands of pilgrims.

19

SOUTHWEST AND SOUTH COAST

Negombo, Kalutara, Beruwala and Bentota,
Ambalangoda, Hikkaduwa, Galle,
Unawatuna, Weligama, Matara,
Tangalla, Hambantota, Yala National Park

Sri Lanka's biggest tourist magnet is a golden coastline of almost 300 km (186 miles) of glorious beaches and translucent blue ocean. Stretching south from Negombo to Hambantota, it boasts a string of attractive resorts from the luxurious to the low-key. All of them offer a wide range of water activities, be it windsurfing, snorkelling among superb coral, or deep-sea fishing. But there are plenty of other things to do, from visiting turtle farms near Bentota and traditional mask carvers in Ambalangoda to exploring the historic Dutch city of Galle.

The best weather along the coast is from November to March. Between May and August you'll face the potential downpours and rough seas of the southwest monsoon, although the sun will often shine for days on end and accommodation will certainly be easier and cheaper to obtain. The tides can be dangerous at times, so watch out for red flag warnings on the beaches.

At Weligama, the fishermen sit patiently on stilts waiting for the tide to bring in the fish.

Negombo

North of Colombo and close to the airport, Negombo is often a first—and last—resort for tourists. The Portuguese settled here early on, and their success at converting the inhabitants is seen in the large number of Catholic churches, earning it the nickname "Little Rome". Easter is an especially important festival, with several passion plays being performed on Duwa Island across the lagoon. But the town is now known mainly for its picturesque fishing boats, traditional outrigger canoes called *oruvas* that bring their catch of prawns and shrimps into the lagoon each morning.

St Mary's Church

The church, begun in 1874 and completed almost 50 years later, dominates the town centre. Its ornate façade and decorated ceiling are particularly impressive.

Fort

A few kilometres south of the town, the original Portuguese fort that overlooked the entrance to the lagoon was reconstructed by the Dutch. Today only the gateway, dated 1678, survives intact.

Canals

As good Dutchmen, the colonists soon set about constructing a series of canals. They were used to shift the spice harvest around more easily, and once ran for 120 km (75 miles) from Colombo in the south to Puttalam in the north. For an enjoyable morning's outing, you can hire a bike in Negombo and ride along the banks.

Kalutara

Around 40 km (25 miles) south of Colombo, Kalutara boasts the best mangosteen fruit in the country. It's also a centre for coir basketware, a by-product of the immense amount of coconut trees that line the coast here. You'll notice, too, that the trees seem to be covered in tourniquets and are linked by tightropes: these are the trappings of the toddy tapper's trade, for the area is Sri Lanka's major producer of arrack.

Gangatilaka Vihara

The large shrine beside the Kalu River is revered by Buddhists for its sacred, spreading bo-tree of the type under which the Buddha meditated. The huge dagoba is, unusually, hollow and has a brightly painted interior.

Beruwala and Bentota

A further 20 km (12 miles) down the coast, these two neighbouring resorts are at the epicentre of Sri Lanka's package-tour industry. They have a range of fine hotels and restaurants, superb beaches and the Bentota River, a perfect lagoon-like spot for windsurfing and sailing. The resorts merge into one another at Alutgama, a

---

KING COCONUT

The humble coconut tree dispenses its riches to Sri Lankans with nothing less than royal largesse, giving them timber, thatch, coir, fruit and palm oil. But some would argue that best of all is the alcohol derived from its sap. Each day for a week, skilled toddy tappers climb up 15 m (50 ft) to the coconut flowers and whack their hard buds with a bone till eventually the sap begins to ooze out. It's collected daily in small clay pots, and to save themselves the trouble of continually clambering up and down trees, the tappers tightrope between them on long strands of coir. The sap is left to ferment on its own to make a sweet, alcoholic toddy, and can then be sent off to be distilled into arrack, a clear spirit with throat-burning strength. The coconut is bountiful to the last: for a great cocktail, mix the arrack with sweet water from the *thambili*—the king coconut.

small town with a famously vibrant fish market and the principal railway station for the resort area.

Kechimalai Mosque

Scenically located on a headland at Beruwala, the mosque marks the landing place of Sri Lanka's first Muslim settlers. The Id-ul-Fitr festival at the end of Ramadan attracts huge numbers of pilgrims.

Bentota River

Boat trips along the calm waters of the Bentota River provide an enjoyable excursion inland when the pleasures of the beach begin to pall. About 5 km (3 miles) upstream is the Galpatha Vihara, a temple dating from the 12th century.

Turtle Hatcheries

The shores stretching south of Bentota are the traditional egg-laying territory of Sri Lanka's five species of turtle. Through a mixture of oceanside development and over-fishing—turtles were hunted for centuries as food and for their beautiful shells—all turtle species have become endangered. Turtle hatcheries have stepped into the breach. They pay fishermen to hand over the eggs and then incubate them till the turtles hatch and can be released into the sea. The oldest estab-lished hatchery is at Kosgoda, but there are now many such places in the area.

Ambalangoda

Ambalangoda, 25 km (16 miles) away, is home to the island's best devil-mask carvers, and some of the shops selling their masks also serve as workshops and museums. There you can watch them being made and see examples of masks that have been used in traditional folk dances.

Hikkaduwa

Hikkaduwa, 13 km (8 miles) to the south, is an increasingly popular tourist resort, with a variety of hotels, restaurants, shops and beaches. It sprawls out along the coast away from the site of the original village but nevertheless manages to retain a good deal of charm. The main attraction is the coral sanctuary, where the coral reefs, and tropical fish and turtles that patrol them, are protected. This is a shallow area whose spectacular sights make for great snorkelling; if you want to be lazy, however, glass-bottomed boats are readily available.

Hikkaduwa also offers such adrenalin-charged watersports as scuba-diving down to shipwrecks and deep coral and surfing: the surf at Wewala and Narigama beaches is good enough to attract an international surfing set.

23

Galle

The historic, fortified city of Galle was Sri Lanka's foremost port until Colombo, some 115 km (70 miles) to the north, was expanded by the British during the 19th century. Legend has it that Galle was the Biblical Tarshish, where the ships of King Solomon loaded gemstones and spices. The next visit of note was in 1505 when the Portuguese arrived. It's said they heard a cock (*galo* in Portuguese) crowing as they entered and named the town after it. They were evicted in 1640 by the Dutch, who constructed a classic red-roofed colonial city surrounded by massive ramparts. Luckily, it is still largely intact. Galle remains an important port, but above all it's a great spot to soak up the old colonial atmosphere of Dutch "Ceilon".

Ramparts

A stroll along the top of the ramparts is one of the special highlights of Galle, and particularly pleasurable at the cooler ends of the day.

Built in the 1660s and punctuated with great bastions, the ramparts offer superb views over both the ocean and the town. The most heavily fortified portion, facing inland, consists of three bastions, Star, Moon and Sun. From the high Moon Bastion, Galle's terracotta roofs and colonial churches can be admired in all their glory.

Follow the wall southeastwards to the Old Gate, topped on the outside by the British royal insignia and inside with the year of its construction, 1669, and the crest of the VOC—the Dutch East India Company.

To the south, on the ocean-facing ramparts, there's a modern lighthouse, while further along, Flag Rock is where the Dutch used an earlier technique of warning ships to steer clear of the rocks—a man would stand here waving a flag. Needless to say, this section is particularly popular at sunset.

National Museum

From the fort's main gate, turn left onto Church Street. Housed in a slightly dilapidated Dutch storehouse of the late 17th century, the museum displays a small but interesting collection of Dutch-period coins, weapons and furniture together with Sinhalese artefacts such as betel-bags, tiles and masks.

New Oriental Hotel

Next door to the museum, the NOH, as it's familiarly known, is an impressive three-storeyed colonial mansion built in 1684 as the Dutch governor's residence and converted to a hotel in the 1860s. The walls are covered

The best feature of Negombo's beach is its fleet of colourful outrigger canoes.

with old maps and pictures, and afternoon tea on the verandah is an unmissable Galle institution.

Groote Kerk
The nearby Dutch Reformed Church, dating from 1752–55, contains the tombs of British as well as Dutch colonial officers. The floor is paved with monumental gravestones from earlier churches.

All Saints Church
Galle's Anglican church is a short distance away on the same street. It was built in the 1860s after the British population had complained about having to worship

at the Groote Kerk, and was consecrated in 1871.

Around Galle
On the corner of Church Street and Queen's Street, opposite a clock tower dating from 1707, the former Dutch Government House has a town crest—a red cockerel—and the year 1683 over the door. It's said to be haunted by the unhappy ghost of a young woman betrayed by her Dutch lover.

Follow Queen's Street, then turn right onto Leyn Baan Street. A few hundred metres on the left is the Dutch Period Museum, a superbly restored colonial-era 25 townhouse. Further along, where Leyn Baan Street meets the ramparts, you come to the old Muslim quarter, with an attractive, twin-towered white mosque.

Unawatuna

The Dutch colonists built their country houses beyond Galle near this beautiful sweeping bay. Today, it's a fairly quiet beach resort with good snorkelling and scuba-diving and plenty of shipwrecks off the coast to provide interest. During the October to March full moons, sea turtles return to the beach to lay their eggs.

Weligama

Just offshore at several points along the coast around Ahangama and Weligama, south of Galle, you may come across stilt fishermen, sitting or standing tirelessly on all-but-submerged poles and casting their lines into the sea. Weligama itself has a wonderful horseshoe bay, with a rocky islet close to the shore. The house peeping through the trees was built by a French count and can be rented—at a price. You'll find exquisite hand-made lacework on sale in the town, a craft in which Weligama specializes.

Matara

Matara, 15 km (9 miles) away, is a large, busy market town at the end of the line for trains going south from Colombo. It was once an Arab trading post and later became a major Dutch stronghold protecting the profitable cinnamon and elephant trade. The old town was easy to secure, situated on a narrow spit of land with the Nilwala River on one side and the ocean on the other. Just to be sure, the Dutch built two forts to do the job.

Star Fort

This small fort in the shape of a six-pointed star is located on the mainland and guarded the bridge to the old town. It was built by the governor, Baron Van Eck, whose name features above the fine gate, along with the VOC crest and date, 1763.

Old Fort

The main fort, just across the Nilwala River, originally enclosed most of the old town, a pleasant area of shaded streets with several fine colonial-era houses. The gateway and some of the ramparts remain. Across from the gate, the red-roofed Dutch Reformed Church dates from 1767.

Dondra Head

A few kilometres from the town and visible from its beach, Dondra is Sri Lanka's southernmost point. An octagonal lighthouse built in 1899 marks the spot.

Tangalla

Another 35 km (22 miles) of delightful coastline brings you to one of the most beautiful resorts in the south. Tangalla's shoreline is the stuff that dreams are made of, divided into a series of intimate little sandy bays that go on into the distance. Apart from the beaches, there are some interesting remnants of the town's colonial past. The charming Tangalla Rest House, overlooking the harbour, was built in 1774 and once housed Dutch officials.

Hambantota

Although Hambantota is only 42 km (26 miles) away, the journey involves a major change in scenery, as you cross from the lush greenery of the wet zone to the dry zone.

Hambantota has a large population of Malay Muslims, who settled in the small fishing port during the colonial era. The big money-spinner isn't fish, though, but salt. The old technique of gathering salt from sea water is still used; the water is slowly evaporated in shallow pans out in the baking-hot sun. You can't miss these large, rectangular pans—their piles of distilled salt are dazzlingly white.

Outside town on the way to Tissamaharama, roadside stalls sell the local delicacy—pots of fresh curds and honey.

Wildlife

Hambantota is a good base for exploring the coast's excellent birdwatching locations. A few kilometres away, the Malala Lewaya lagoon attracts several species of water birds—and crocodiles too. Further along, the Bundala Bird Sanctuary is home to fleets of flamingoes, pelicans and spoonbills. At certain times of the year, wild elephants can be spotted.

Yala National Park

Also called Ruhuna National Park, Sri Lanka's major elephant reserve is 40 km (25 miles) from Hambantota. The best season is from October to December—the drier the weather, the fewer the waterholes, which in turn attract more animals. But you never know what might turn up early or late in the day: buffalo, deer, wild boar, or even—if you're extremely lucky—a leopard. The bird life is spectacular, notably peacocks, pelicans, storks and spoonbills.

Kataragama

On the western edge of the park, this attractive town is home to a remarkable Hindu festival during the July/August full moon, when thousands of pilgrims attend the temple. The festival is rounded off with amazing acts of firewalking and body-piercing, carried out as penance by pilgrims.

KANDY AND THE HILL COUNTRY
Kandy, Nuwara Eliya, Around the Hill Country

The range of mountains within which the kingdom of Kandy was able to remain independent during centuries of colonial rule is without doubt the most visually stunning region of Sri Lanka. Escarpments over 1,000 m (3,280 ft) high rise sheer out of the coastal plains, providing a spectacular journey up by car or train, with dramatic views at every turn.

Along with the grandeur of the scenery there's the fascinating ancient Sinhalese capital of Kandy itself, plus nearby botanical gardens and an elephant orphanage, the colonial hill station of Nuwara Eliya, and a chance to visit one of the many tea plantations that dominate the landscape.

Kandy

Sri Lanka's second-biggest city became the capital of a separate kingdom in the 15th century, and after the fall of Kotte in 1597 was the last preserve of Sinhalese independence. Kandy resisted Portuguese and Dutch attempts at conquest, finally falling to the British in 1815 when the last king

The Temple of the Tooth stands in the centre of a moated compound by the lakeside.

was captured and exiled. It has remained the country's cultural and spiritual centre to this day, however, due to the presence here of Sri Lanka's most important religious site, the Temple of the Tooth. The temple is the centrepiece of the annual *Esala Perahera*, culminating in the tremendous torchlight procession of elephants, dancers and musicians. Meanwhile, the exuberant Kandyan dance is performed at various venues around town throughout the year.

The Lake

At the heart of Kandy lies this beautiful artificial lake, created in 1807 by the last king, Sri Vikrama Rajasinha. It took the forced labour of at least 3,000 men to achieve and, along with the king's other extravagances, was partly the reason why his disaffected nobles encouraged the British to depose him. The island in the middle was his personal pleasure garden; the pragmatic British later used it as an ammunition dump. A circuit of the lake covers a scenic 4 km (2.5 miles).

Temple of the Tooth

On the lake's northern shore stands the Dalada Maligawa, as the temple is formally known. It occupies a large compound, with buildings dating mainly from the 17th and 18th centuries. The octagonal tower and deep moat that surrounds it are courtesy of King Rajasinha. Either side of the lakeside gate are two fine elephant carvings.

The tooth in question is the Buddha's, which is supposed to have been rescued from his funeral pyre and brought to the island in the 4th century AD hidden in the hair of an Indian princess. It is without question Sri Lanka's most hallowed relic. As such, it's long been the target of those wishing to undermine Sinhalese independence: the Tamils took the holy relic back to India in the 13th century, and the British seized it as part of their plan to capture Kandy. Now it reposes on a golden lotus blossom in the smallest of seven caskets each inside a larger one, heavily guarded by monks.

The room housing the shrine which contains the tooth is opened at 5.30 and 9.30 a.m. and 6.30 p.m. Then, to a beating of drums, clashing of cymbals and wailing of flutes, pilgrims with lotus blossoms and fragrant frangipani approach the shrine. A curtain is drawn aside to reveal only the outermost golden casket.

Note that since a bomb attack in 1998 the temple has heavy security and is only open to visitors from 6 a.m. to 5 p.m. (though it's a good idea to arrive well before closing time).

National Museum

Located in the former Queen's Palace behind the temple, the museum displays a fine collection of Kandyan costumes, jewellery, royal regalia, palm-leaf books, weapons, tools and devil masks, documenting Sinhalese life before the Europeans arrived on the scene.

3 **THE THREE BEST COLONIAL EXPERIENCES** The days of empire may be gone, but its gracious lifestyle can still be sampled. In **Galle**, wander along Dutch-built ramparts overlooking the ocean and cool off with a drink at the former Dutch governor's residence. The British Empire lives on in the hill station of **Nuwara Eliya**, with its golf course, mock-Tudor architecture and old-fashioned Hill Club. Back in **Colombo**, retire to the 19th-century splendour of the Galle Face Hotel for afternoon tea on the verandah.

St Paul's Church
In Palace Square, on the town side of the temple, the Anglican St Paul's Church dates from 1843. Its interior has several interesting memorials and plaques. Note also the square's fountain decorated with cherubs and fish; it was erected by the coffee planters of Ceylon in 1875 to commemorate the visit of the Prince of Wales (later Edward VII) just as their industry was on the point of collapse.

Royal Palace Park
Over on the southwest corner of the lake, steps lead up to Royal Palace Park, another of King Rajasinha's creations, and also called Wace Park. There are good views over the lake, but the centrepiece is a Japanese cannon captured in World War II and given as a present by Lord Mountbatten, Commander-in-Chief of the Allied forces in Asia. His wartime headquarters were in the venerable old Swiss Hotel, towards the eastern end of the lake.

Peradeniya Botanic Gardens
Situated within a loop of the Mahaweli River 6 km (4 miles) outside Kandy, the gardens cover some 60 ha (148 acres) and contain thousands of species of plants, trees and flowers. Huge clumps of giant bamboo shoot up more than 30 m (100 ft) along the river, and there's a magnificent avenue of Royal Palms. The gardens also boast such exotic vegetation as tamarind, jasmine and tilting Cook's Pines, as well as an orchid house and spice groves. Most spectacular of all is the Giant Java fig tree *(Ficus benjaminus)* on the Great Lawn, whose branches spread out over 1,800 sq m (20,000 sq ft).

Three Temples
Just beyond the Botanic Gardens, you can head out along a minor road into rural Sri Lanka, passing rice paddies and small villages, to three delightful temples dating from the 14th century.

Gadaladeniya temple has excellent 600-year-old frescoes beneath the dagoba, and a beautifully decorated jackwood door giving access to the Hindu-influenced shrine.

A short distance away, Lankatilaka sits on a rocky outcrop with magnificent views of the surrounding hills. The three-tiered temple, reached by steps cut in the rock, has a typical Kandyan-style sloping roof and is ringed by elephant sculptures.

It's another 3 km (2 miles) to Embekke Devale, whose marvellous wooden audience hall is carved with soldiers, musicians, wrestlers, Kandyan dancers and double-headed eagles.

Pinnawela Elephant Orphanage

Harbouring more than 50 abandoned animals, this government-run orphanage is probably the best chance to see elephants en masse: running loose on the orphanage's open field, they make an imposing sight. The most popular spectacle is feeding time, when a circle of cute baby giants drink from outsize milk bottles. This takes place at 9.15 a.m., 1.15 and 5.15 p.m.

Nuwara Eliya

The Nuwara Eliya highlands stand at the top of a dizzying zig-zag road nearly 80 km (50 miles) south of Kandy. It was first established in the 19th century as a hill station by British colonial officials and tea planters who found sanctuary in its cool climate—and at 1,889 m (6,200 ft), you'll need to come equipped for nights that can get downright cold. The town was built after the British explorer Sir Samuel Baker arrived here in 1846 and decided it was a perfect place to recreate England in the tropics.

Today, the centre of town looks like most others in Sri Lanka, and it's very popular with the jet set from Colombo who

Each tiny tea leaf is carefully plucked by hand.

come here in April for horse-racing and endless parties. But Samuel Baker's slice of the old country is still visible around its edges in the magnificently incongruous architecture, which ranges from mock-Tudor to Scottish baronial. There's also an immaculate 18-hole golf course, trout-stocked Gregory's Lake, an Anglican church with an old graveyard and a twee pink brick village post office. The Hill Club, with its billiard room, photos of the Queen and strict rules requiring male guests to wear jacket and tie after 7 p.m., reflects the attitudes of a bygone era.

Mount Pidurutalagala

If you find the bracing air and colonial atmosphere has quickened the spirit, you can always go for a walk up Sri Lanka's highest mountain. Mt Pidurutalagala's 2,524-m (8,281-ft) peak looms over the town and is often under cloud. But when it's not, the views from the top are stunning, taking in all the hill country and stretching as far as the ocean.

Tea Plantations

Nuwara Eliya is surrounded by tea plantations. Tea thrives on high, sloping terrain and sunny weather, all of which this area has in abundance. The bushes are distinctively small and neat but if left unpruned would grow to 33

30 m (100 ft) in height. The pickers are all women and come mainly from the Tamil community. Basketloads of bright green leaves and buds are brought to the factories to undergo a five-stage process of drying, rolling, sifting, fermentation and firing, all of which reduces 100 kg (220 lb) of green leaves to 25 kg (55 lb) of black tea.

CEYLON TEA

The Dutch came to Sri Lanka for its famous spices, but the country is now more associated with an imported plant—tea. Sri Lanka is the world's third largest tea-producing nation after China and India; tea exports are the backbone of the economy. In fact, it's all courtesy of *Hemileia vastatrix*, a leaf disease that wiped out the once-booming coffee industry in the 1870s and boosted tea into pole position. The first plantation in Sri Lanka had only been set up a few years earlier in 1867 at the Lollecondera Estate as an experiment to see whether tea would grow on the island. The experiment was a resounding success, and the face of the country was changed beyond recognition. As you drive around the hill country today, you'll see lush green tea bushes carpeting the mountainsides.

Guided plantation tours at such places as Labookellie Tea Centre and Glen Loch are a fascinating and informative introduction to the subject of tea, and end, of course, with a cup of Sri Lanka's finest.

Hakgala Botanical Garden

This very pleasant garden, about 10 km (6 miles) southeast of Nuwara Eliya, has wild orchids, roses, a Japanese garden and a plant house. Hakgala means "jaw rock" and features in Hindu legend as the place where Hanuman, the monkey-god, ripped out a piece of rock with his mouth in order to bring the special herbs growing on it back to Rama.

Around the Hill Country

The less sweltering temperatures of the Hill Country allow you to enjoy the great outdoors in comfort, but bear in mind that the cooler air can be deceptive—the sun burns just as powerfully up here. There are enjoyable walks and scenically positioned rest houses. The region is also the centre of Sri Lanka's gem-mining industry.

Ratnapura

Just to the southwest of the Hill Country, and with fine views of Adam's Peak, Ratnapura is the nation's gem capital (its name literally means "city of gems"). It seems at times that the entire population is in the business of selling stones, though many of the offerings will be fake. You can begin your education at the Gem Bank Gemmological Museum, a short way out of town on the road to Badulla.

Adam's Peak

Sri Lanka's sacred mountain, 2,224 m (7,300 ft) high, derives its name in both English and Sinhalese (Sri Pada or "Sacred Footprint") from the footprint-shaped indentation in the rock at the very top. All Sri Lanka's major religions claim it was made by their man, be it Adam, the Buddha or Shiva, and as a result it's a hugely important pilgrimage site.

From Dalhousie, countless steps lead 7 km (4 miles) up to the peak, a three- to four-hour walk. Many do it in the early hours of the morning in order to reach the top at sunrise, a magical moment when a vast shadow of the triangular peak is projected onto the mist, and then moves back eerily towards the viewer as the sun rises and the mist recedes.

The climbing season is from December to April, when thousands of pilgrims make the ascent. The summit, complete with temple, is a holy site and no matter how cold you feel, you must approach it minus shoes and hat. Luckily, there are plenty of tea houses open on the way up for hot drinks and snacks, and where you will also be able to rest for part of the night.

Horton Plains and World's End

This marvellous, remote plateau more than 2,000 m (6,500 ft) high provides Sri Lanka's most memorable hiking terrain. There are some great trails leading through grassland and forest and surrounded by mountains. The most famous leads 4.5 km (2.8 miles) from Farr's Inn rest house to the remarkable World's End, where the Hill Country suddenly stops at a 1,312-m 4,300-ft) precipice. It's best seen early in the morning when the air is clear and the views of the southern coastal plains are a wonder.

Ella

If you're keen on getting breathtaking views without going to the trouble of hiking across the Horton Plains, then head to Ella on the eastern side of the Hill Country. Here, at the Ella Gap, the escarpment, 1,000 m (3,280 ft) high, splits apart and the valley plummets to the plains below, with views all the way to the Yala National Park. Happily, the whole panorama is best seen from the comfort of the Ella Rest House terrace, where food and drinks are also served.

ANCIENT CITIES
Anuradhapura, Mihintale, Aukana,
Polonnaruwa, Sigiriya, Dambulla

Sinhalese civilization first rose to prominence in the great Anuradhapuran kingdom of the northern plains some 2,500 years ago. But the island's rulers were forced to move their capital ever southwards in order to secure it from successive attacks by south Indian invaders. Over the centuries the jungle reclaimed these abandoned cities, and even with the archaeological care lavished on them in recent times they retain the mysterious grandeur of lost civilizations. First and foremost, though, they are testament to the towering confidence and cultural dynamism of Sri Lanka's early Buddhist society.

Anuradhapura
Founded in the 5th century BC, Sri Lanka's first great capital became both the political and religious centre of the nation a century later, when it was converted to Buddhism under King Tissa. In its heyday Anuradhapura was a wonder of civic buildings and temples, with an elaborate irrigation system, before beginning a

At Gal Vihara in Polonnaruwa, the reclining image of Buddha entering nirvana.

steady decline 1,000 years ago. By the time archaeologists rediscovered it in the 19th century it was deserted. A modern market town has developed a few kilometres away from the ancient one, providing a base for most of Anuradhapura's many visitors.

Twin Ponds
At the northern end of the ancient city, these ritual baths, Kuttam Pokuna, were filled via an extensive system of underground pipes. The water spout is in the top corner of the smaller pond, with a carved five-headed cobra next to it.

Samadhi Buddha
Nearby, the 3rd–4th century AD sculpture of a meditating Buddha is by common consent one of the finest statues of its kind in Asia.

Abhayagiri Dagoba
When it was built in the 1st century BC, this enormous dagoba, 100 m (328 ft) high, just west of the Samadhi Buddha, towered over a monastery complex with 5,000 monks in residence.

Mahasena Palace
The site of the palace, a few hundred metres to the north, is visited

now chiefly for its moonstone, the highly ornate semi-circular stone found at the entrance to important buildings. This particular example is a high point of early Buddhist art, with exquisite carvings of elephants, horses, lions and bulls in an eternal round of follow-my-leader. In fact, these animals symbolize birth, age, illness and death and represent the cycle of reincarnation that individuals must go through to attain nirvana, embodied by the lotus in the centre of the moonstone.

Ratnaprasada

Outside this ruined 8th-century monastery, look out for the handsome guardstone, the decorative feature placed next to the entrance steps intended to ward off evil. The guardian is crowned with a fearsome seven-headed cobra and is next to a kneeling elephant.

Thuparama Dagoba

In a delightful park-like setting south of Ratnaprasada, Sri Lanka's oldest temple dates from the time of King Tissa's conversion to Buddhism in the 3rd century BC. It was originally built in the paddy-heap shape (i.e. like a heap of fresh harvested rice) to shelter what was said to be the Buddha's collarbone. The current bell shape is the result of 19th-century renovations, while the circle of granite pillars was added in the 7th century and once supported a canopy.

THE CULTURAL TRIANGLE

With its three points located at the ancient capitals of Kandy, Polonnaruwa and Anuradhapura, Sri Lanka's Cultural Triangle includes some of Asia's most remarkable antiquities—five of which have been designated World Heritage Sites by the United Nations. Apart from the three cities, other unmissable sights are the frescoed 5th-century rock fortress at Sigiriya and the superb cave temples at Dambulla. The entrance charges can be quite steep, and if you're planning to visit Anuradhapura, Polonnaruwa and Sigiriya in particular, it's worth investing in a Cultural Triangle Round Ticket. This will save you both time (the ticket offices are sometimes very far away from the sites themselves) as well as money. The ticket is available from offices of the Ceylon Tourist Board or the Central Cultural Fund, 212/1 Bauddhaloka Mawatha, Colombo 7, tel. (1) 500733, fax (1) 500731, e-mail gen_ccf@sri.lanka.net).

Jetawanarama Dagoba

The vast brick dome of the dagoba, a kilometre to the east of Thuparama, stood 130 m (427 ft) high when it was constructed by King Mahasena in the 3rd century AD—as tall as the Great Pyramid in Egypt, though it has subsided a little since then. For some time now it has been undergoing a major UNESCO-funded restoration.

Ruwanweli Saya Dagoba

South of Thuparama, the massive, white dome of the dagoba dazzles the eye in the light of the sun or the moon. It was built under the orders of King Dutugemenu in the 2nd century BC, though he never saw it completed. Legend says that his brother had it covered in white cloth to give the dying king an idea of how magnificent it would one day look. The outer wall is lined with carved elephants, beyond which are some attractive groves.

Brazen Palace

Continue south along a very pleasant avenue. To the left of the path you'll notice a forest of pillars. They once held up the first floor of a nine-storey monastic building with a bronze roof (which gave the palace its name). The palace dates from Dutugemenu's reign in the 2nd century BC, although the 1,600 pillars that remain are part of a 12th-century revamp by the Polonnaruwan king, Parakramabahu I.

Sacred Bo-Tree (Sri Maha Bodhi)

A short distance away is one of Sri Lanka's most venerated objects, the Sacred Bo-Tree grown from a cutting of the same one under which the Buddha attained enlightenment. The cutting was brought here from northern India 2,200 years ago by Sanghamitta, daughter of the great Buddhist emperor Ashoka, and tended by guardians ever since. Surrounded by shrines and protected by a golden railing put up in 1966, the tree is a living connection to the founder of Buddhism and attracts countless pilgrims.

Isurumuniya Vihara

Located to the south of the ancient city, the 3rd-century BC temple is reached via a bridge over a lotus pond. It's carved out of a large rock, which you can climb for views that are especially good at sunset. The outline of frolicking elephants can be seen etched into the rock overlooking the pool next to the shrine. Be sure to visit the temple's small museum, containing some excellent sculptures. Best known of all is the marvellous Gupta Lovers, dating from around the 5th century AD.

39

Archaeological Museum

The museum, near the Ruwan-weli Saya Dagoba, is housed in an attractive colonial building. There are displays of the various types of Buddhist shrines, a roomful of bronze statues and collections of pottery, coins, jewellery boxes and other archaeological finds from around Anuradhapura. A golden casket is said to hold the remains of the country's first hero-king, Dutugemenu, who defeated the Tamils in the 2nd century BC. Top marks for the unexpected, though, goes to an intriguing set of urinals and squatting plates outside the main building, sculpted by monks in the 5th and 6th centuries AD.

Mihintale

Mihintale, 11 km (7 miles) east of the ancient capital, is of huge significance to Sri Lankans as the place where King Tissa met Mahinda, son of the Emperor Ashoka and persuasive Buddhist missionary. The king was converted to Buddhism and the rest, as they say, is history.

At the top of the 1,840 granite stairs, the spot where the meeting occurred is marked by the Sela Cetiya, a small dagoba surrounded by crowned pillars. Up a

The Aukana Buddha is joined at the back to the rock face.

steep path to the right is the large, white Mahaseya Dagoba, which tradition says was built to contain Mahinda's relics. The views from here are breathtaking, with the great dagobas of Anuradhapura clearly visible in the distance. Other viewpoints are the "anointing rock", whose summit is reached via a precarious path, and "Mahinda's bed", a lump of rock where the missionary is said to have rested before changing the course of Sri Lankan civilization forever.

Aukana

Around 40 km (25 miles) south of Mihintale, a scenic backroad leads you to the impressive Aukana Buddha. The road runs part of the way alongside the vast Kalawewa tank which, like the statue, was built during the reign of King Dhatusena in the 5th century AD. The 13-m (43-ft) Buddha, carved out of the hillside's solid rock, counts among Asia's finest. It's seen to best advantage in the morning, when the first rays of the sun strike its serene, full-lipped face. It's an intentional effect of the sculptors and gives this statue its name—the word *aukana* means "sun-eater".

Polonnaruwa

Following repeated invasions from south India, the Sinhalese kings abandoned Anuradhapura 41 in the 11th century for a site further inland. Remarkably, the new capital at Polonnaruwa reached even greater heights of artistic and architectural excellence, and mostly within the reign of just two kings, Parakramabahu I and Nissankamalla. By the 13th century the golden age was over, as the city finally succumbed to south Indian armies.

Polonnaruwa covers a large area filled with palaces, temples and parks and is beautifully situated next to Parakramabahu's greatest achievement, a reservoir so vast it was given the title of Parakrama Samudra—"Parakrama's Sea".

South of the City
A short walk south of the Ancient City is the circular Potgul Vihara, thought to have been used as a library, around which are four small dagobas. Nearby is the fine statue of, probably, King Parakramabahu carrying a rope that's been interpreted as representing the yoke-like burdens of kingship.

Royal Citadel
From the main, reservoir-side entrance to the Ancient City, turn right onto the dirt road, which leads to Parakramabahu's mighty palace complex. The imposing Royal Palace was said to have been seven storeys tall with 1,000 rooms—note the formidable walls, 3.5 m (10 ft) thick. Across from the palace, the outside of Parakramabahu's Audience Hall is decorated with superb elephant and lion friezes. Just beyond is a bathing pool, with two crocodile-head water spouts.

4 **THE FOUR BEST FESTIVALS** Sri Lanka is a land of colourful year-round festivals. January sees Colombo's biggest festivities at the **Kelaniya Temple**, celebrating the Buddha's visit there over 2,000 years ago. In June, the myriad stairs at **Mihintale** are ascended by thousands of pilgrims dressed in white. The biggest of all the festivals is the 10-day **Esala Perahera** held in Kandy during the July/August full moon and featuring drummers, dancers and a hundred brightly decorated elephants. Also at this time, the Hindu festival at **Katagarama** is a riot of brilliant processions, music, dancing and fire-walking.

Shiva Devale I

Return along the same road to this beautiful Hindu temple. It was built in the early 13th century, at a time of increasing south Indian influence in the kingdom.

Vatadage

Beyond the temple is a walled compound known as the Quadrangle, banked up 4 m (13 ft) high and containing a remarkable number of 12th-century buildings. The Vatadage, a circular relic house, is its high point. Four intricately carved stone stairways, a Buddha statue at the top of each, lead to the main hall. The building itself has superb friezes, and the moonstone and guardstones at the foot of the northern stairway are especially fine.

Thuparama

Behind the Vatadage, in the southwest corner of the Quadrangle, this image house dates from the reign of Parakramabahu and contains some old statues. It's mainly of interest, though, as the only such building retaining its traditional vaulted roof.

Hatadage

Immediately opposite the Vatadage, the Hatadage was built by King Nissankamalla as a temple of the tooth, and the Tooth Relic (now in Kandy) may have been kept here at some point.

Satmahal Prasada

The six-storey pyramidal tower near the Hatadage is in an unusual style for Sri Lanka and may show early links with the architecture of other Buddhist nations, such as Thailand and Cambodia.

Galpotha

Lying on the eastern side of the Hatadage, the enormous stone "book" of edicts and lavish praise for Nissankamalla is the ultimate in heavy reading. According to an inscription, the 25-tonne slab was hauled here from Mihintale, more than 100 km (60 miles) away, by elephants.

Rankot Vihara

An impressive group of buildings 1.5 km (a mile) north of the Quadrangle forms part of the Alahana Parivena—the Royal Cremation Monastery, erected on grounds set aside for cremation by Parakramabahu. The monumentally proportioned Rankot Vihara, with a fine restored spire, was built by Nissankamalla and measures 55 m (180 ft) tall and 170 m (558 ft) in circumference, making it the largest structure in Polonnaruwa.

Baddhasima Pasada

The monks' convocation hall stands half a kilometre to the north. It's located on the highest ground in the city and has good

views over the encroaching jungle. The Chief Abbot's throne is still visible in the centre.

Lankatilaka

A path leads to the nearby five-storey Lankatilaka. At 17 m (56 ft) high, made entirely from brick and with a central nave, it looks oddly like a cathedral. It was built by Parakramabahu to house a huge statue of the Buddha, whose eroded form still stands at the far end of the aisle.

Kiri Vihara

The name of this dagoba, just to the north, is not the original one and means "milk-white shrine". When the area was excavated after centuries of neglect, the 12th-century dagoba was found to be in pristine condition.

Gal Vihara

From Kiri Vihara, cross the road to one of Sri Lanka's greatest attractions. The four giant Buddhas of Gal Vihara were part of Parakramabahu's northern monastery and are undoubtedly the supreme achievement of Polonnaruwan sculpture. They are carved out of a single granite boulder, and the beautiful grain of the rock only adds to their effect.

Handsome guardstones flank the stairways of the Vatadage.

The first two Buddhas are seated, though the second one, in a hollow in the rock, is obscured behind a perspex window. The crowning glory, however, is the next pair of statues. The expressive power achieved in the standing Buddha has rightly been marvelled at, with its rare crossed-arms stance and a profound look of compassion and strength in the face. The 14-m (46-ft) reclining statue shows the Buddha attaining enlightenment as he passes from the world. The genius is in the detail, with subtle touches like the flowing lines of the robe and the pillow slightly indented with the weight of the head.

North of Gal Vihara

A short way from Gal Vihara, the vast Demala Mahaseya, a pet project of Parakramabahu, was on course for becoming the biggest dagoba in the land until it was abandoned. The labourers were Tamils taken prisoner during the king's retaliatory attacks on southern India. Northwest of here is the delightful Lotus Pond, a stone pool shaped like a lotus flower. Carved during the reign of King Nissankamalla, it's a quintessential Buddhist gesture.

Further on, the Tivanka Image House is a large brick structure with a fine set of 12th-century frescoes and a "thrice-bent" Buddha—that is, curved at the shoulder, waist and knee and possibly intended to suggest the feminine form.

Archaeological Museum

The new, purpose-built museum is located near the reservoir. It's nicely laid out, with informative maps, photos and panels that put the sites of the ancient city in their historical and cultural contexts. The finds on display, with some superb Buddhist and Hindu sculptures from around Polonnaruwa, are excellent.

Polonnaruwa, like most Sri Lankan towns, has a comfortable rest house in an old colonial building. This one boasts a verandah overlooking the lake with a view across to the peaks of the hill country.

Sigiriya

Sigiriya—Lion Rock—is a massive, square-shaped block of granite, 180 m (600 ft) high that rises dramatically out of the jungle. With its commanding views and sheer walls, it's a natural citadel, which is why it attracted King Kasyapa I in the 5th century. Having usurped the throne by murdering his father, King Dhatusena, he then feared for his own life, and fled here from Anuradhapura. Sigiriya became Sri Lanka's capital until his death in AD 495. In that time Kasyapa built a magnificent fortress-cum-palace on top of the rock, and delightful water gardens.

It's a hot, tough climb to the top—Kasyapa would never have settled here if it was easy—but the effort is more than repaid by the results, a set of brilliant frescoes halfway up, and wonderful 360° views of the surrounding country from the ruined palace.

Frescoes

In a small cavity in the western side of the rock are the famous 5th-century frescoes of voluptuous, almond-eyed celestial maidens emerging out of the clouds. There were once 500, but only 21 have survived the centuries of sun and rain. The subtle yellow, orange and green paintwork is beautiful, and the effect they had on their early male viewers was remarkable. On Mirror Wall, just below the frescoes, 7th–11th-century graffiti record the poetic and often steamy thoughts of those first tourists.

Royal Palace

Continue up the path by Mirror Wall till you come to Lion Terrace. Kasyapa had a giant brick lion built here as the forbidding gateway to his fortress, which would have been entered through the lion's mouth. Now all that's left are the great lion paws on either side of the staircase leading upwards.

The monolith of Lion Rock seems naturally designed for a citadel.

The ruins of Kasyapa's mighty palace cover the 1.5-ha (3.7-acre) summit, testament to the grandeur of his vision. Most poignant of all is his huge throne, hewn out of the granite and looking east across the plains to the rising sun.

Dambulla

The Dambulla caves tunnel into a huge rock 160 m (525 ft) high, 19 km (12 miles) southwest of Sigiriya. They were also used as a refuge by a fleeing Anuradhapuran monarch. King Valagambahu spent 14 years holed up in them in the 1st century BC, escaping an invasion from India. After he regained his throne, he had this wonderful rock temple constructed as a mark of gratitude.

The five caves are fronted by a colonnaded verandah, and sit beneath a rock that sweeps up like a great wave. The first contains a 14-m (46-ft) reclining Buddha carved out of the rock. Most impressive of them all, however, is the second one. Completely ringed by statues of Hindu gods as well as the Buddha, and with 15th–18th-century frescoes covering every inch of the cave ceiling, it's an amazing assault on the senses. The views from outside the caves are equally splendid, with the rock fortress of Sigiriya visible across the plain.

At present, visits to Sri Lanka's remote north and beautiful east coast are discouraged, although Trincomalee is open to foreign visitors. Tour guides and hired drivers probably won't take you there, but there are regular train and bus services. Nevertheless, it's a good idea to obtain up-to-the-minute advice from the Ceylon Tourist Board and registering with your embassy in Colombo before setting off.

Both the east coast and the northern Jaffna peninsula—where the Tamil population is concentrated—have been major areas of conflict between the Tamil Tigers and the Sri Lankan army since the early 1980s. Things are relatively calm at the time of writing and both sides have felt able to include the word "peace" in their vocabularies. However, nothing can be taken for granted in both these parts of the country.

When the situation is finally settled, though, the vast, wildlife-packed Wilpattu National Park, Jaffna's splendid Dutch fort—the best in the island—and such marvellous east coast locations as Batticaloa and Arugam Bay, Sri Lanka's most famous surfing spot, will once again be must-sees on the tourist itinerary.

Trincomalee

Trinco, as it's known to its friends, sits on the northern tip of Koddiyar Bay, one of the world's great natural harbours. This is where the first Tamils arrived in Sri Lanka over 2,000 years ago, and later it was a port of call for all the great European navies, with such famous visitors as Lord Nelson and the Duke of Wellington admiring its size and beauty. The town is very battered but still has some interesting sights; it is the starting point for trips to fine nearby beaches.

Fort Frederick

The fort named after the Duke of York in 1803 occupies a spit of land east of the town. Originally built by the Portuguese in 1624, it changed hands numerous times over the following centuries between the Dutch, British and French, eventually falling into the possession of the British again; many of their military buildings still exist, and you can still see the cannon emplacements. The fort is now run by the Sri Lankan army who, in the light of the current troubles, sometimes forbid entry to visitors.

The Dutch-built gatehouses date from 1676. If you can get past them, you will see, some way along the road to the right, a large verandahed building. This is Wellesley House, where the Duke of Wellington convalesced in 1799 after the Tipu Sultan wars in India.

Swami Rock

The road continues as far as Swami ("the Lord's") Rock at the end of the peninsula. Nearby is a brightly painted Hindu temple dedicated to Shiva, Koneswaram Kovil, built in the 1960s. An earlier temple on this site, dating from the 3rd century, was tipped into the ocean by the Portuguese when they arrived in 1624. Two bronze sculptures and the temple's lingam, symbolizing Shiva, have since been found by divers and returned to the new temple. The views of the bay from the terrace are superb.

Beaches

Just a few kilometres north of Trinco, Uppuveli is a pleasant beach that's within walking distance from the town. A further 10 km (6 miles) brings you to one of the best beaches in the country. Nilaveli has a beautiful expanse of white-sand beach stretching for no less than 30 km (18 miles), fringed with palm trees and ending at a lagoon.

Offshore, Pigeon Island takes its name from the Blue Rock pigeons which nest here. It's a good place for snorkelling and diving around the excellent coral reef, although at the moment it might prove difficult obtaining a boat in which to get there.

If you bathe along this coast, watch out for sting rays, sea urchins and jellyfish that come close to shore in late July.

5 THE BEST FIVE BEACHES With their golden sands, sapphire seas and palm fringes, Sri Lanka's beaches are idyllic. Here is our recommended selection: watch picturesque outrigger canoes bringing in their catch on the beach at **Negombo**; at **Hikkaduwa**, swim out to see fascinating coral reef and technicolour tropical fish; **Weligama** occupies a stunning horseshoe bay, where traditional stilt fishermen perch out at sea; endless gleaming white-sand beaches and an easy-going pace make **Tangalla** the perfect place to unwind; beautiful **Nilaveli**, just north of Trincomalee, stretches 4 km (2.5 miles) and ends at a deep blue lagoon.

CULTURAL NOTES

Bandaranaike

The Bandaranaike name is a potent force in Sri Lanka: the international airport, museums, conference centres and streets all bear the moniker of the nation's most charismatic political family. It began with the rise to power of Solomon Bandaranaike, an Oxford-educated lawyer born in Colombo in 1899. Bandaranaike was part of the conservative UNP government after independence, but quit to found the nationalist SLFP. He became prime minister in 1956, with policies committed to replacing English with Sinhala as the official language and promoting Buddhism in the affairs of state. Some may argue this led to the disaffection of the minority Tamils, a problem that continues with terrible consequences to this day, but Bandaranaike, who was assassinated by a disgruntled Buddhist monk in 1959, remains a hero to the majority of ordinary Sinhalese. So much so, in fact, that his widow, Sirimavo Bandaranaike, was invited to head the SLFP after his death, and became the world's first woman prime minister following the 1960 general election. Their daughter, Chandrika Bandaranaike Kumaratunga, has continued in the family business by being elected president in 1994.

Buddhism

The religion was founded in India 2,500 years ago by Siddhartha Gautama, a prince who attained spiritual enlightenment after seven weeks' meditation under the bo-tree (thereby acquiring the name Buddha, which means "enlightened one" in Sanskrit). Its complex philosophy sees life as a state of suffering and stresses the need for individuals to overcome this by extinguishing personal desire and seeking the perfect, enlightened detachment of nirvana, something that may take several reincarnations to achieve.

Buddhism was brought to Sri Lanka in 247 BC with the conversion of King Tissa at Mihintale. Intriguingly, whereas the religion was overwhelmed by Hinduism in India, it took root and flourished in Sri Lanka. It's fair to say that it has been the bedrock of Sinhalese culture ever since. Buddhism was the fixed point on which the great civilizations at Anuradhapura and Polonnaruwa were built, and on which Sri Lankan identity was later maintained through the long centuries of Indian and

European conquest. Its physical expression—an array of magnificent and beautiful temples, ancient cities, statues and paintings that stretch back over two millennia—is an ever-present reminder of its position at the heart of Sri Lankan culture.

Cricket

Sometimes, it seems, to understand Sri Lanka you must get to grips with its obsession with cricket. More than just the national sport, it's also a vital cultural glue that helps keep this often fractured country together. This was never more evident than during the 1996 Cricket World Cup played in south Asia. Not merely tournament underdogs, Sri Lanka also suffered the indignity of having other teams, most notably Australia, refuse to play in Colombo for reasons of security. When Sri Lanka found itself in the final against the Australians, played in Lahore, Pakistan, the stage was set for unparalleled outbursts of national fervour, and virtually the entire population stopped whatever it was doing to watch TV or listen to the radio commentary. Sri Lanka became World Champions by an unprecedented seven wickets, and the captain Arjuna Ranatunga and his team became instant heroes to Sri Lankans on all sides of the cultural divide. The national pride stimulated by that victory in Lahore has never quite subsided, and Sri Lanka now confidently holds its own on the cricketing world stage.

Kandyan Dance

The distinctive Kandyan dance developed around Buddhist religious ceremonies, but retains strong elements of its very earthy folk roots from a time when villagers worshipped less orthodox gods. The dance combines a twofold assault on the senses: powerful rhythmic drumming and energetic, acrobatic dancers in brilliant costumes and fantastic masks. The men pirouette and somersault, the women move with grace and elegance.

It's a breathtaking spectacle in either of the forms which it now takes. Many visitors will watch it performed as a secular show, and whether in a tourist hotel or at the Kandyan Arts Association theatre, the standard is usually very high. But it might be more satisfying to see it in the appropriate religious setting. Each day, drummers play at Kandy's Temple of the Tooth during the *puja* ceremony, while both musicians and dancers are an essential part of major *poya* festivals, most notably the great *Esala Perahera* held in Kandy during the July/August full moon.

Shopping

Sri Lanka produces eye-catching clothes, jewellery, batik textiles and a variety of superb handicrafts. All are available in the shops and markets of Colombo, but if you travel around the country you'll find an even greater range at the places of manufacture, and always at very reasonable prices.

Where?

In Colombo, the most exciting shopping is to be had in the Pettah, where the teeming, noisy streets packed with wall-to-wall shops selling every kind of product are an unforgettable experience in themselves. Prices are whatever you agree on with the shopkeeper, so be prepared to haggle. Things are more sedate in nearby Fort. The government-owned Laksala shop on York Street has a wide selection of Sri Lankan items on sale. The goods are guaranteed to be genuine and the prices are fixed; the downside is you'll probably pay more because of this.

What?

There is a wide choice of tempting souvenirs. Avoid items made of tortoiseshell, ivory or ebony.

Batik

Originating in Indonesia, batik is an ancient technique of putting patterns on textiles by the complex art of printing with wax and dyes. The Sri Lankans have proved themselves adept batik craftsmen and their attractive designs now adorn such items as clothes, curtains, table cloths, pictures and wall hangings.

Crafts

Sri Lanka's craftsmen are highly skilled and produce marvellous souvenirs in a variety of materials. Coconut shells are turned into carvings, while the coconut fibre (coir) is used to make durable and attractive basketware, bags and mats. Lacquerware bowls, elephants carved in everything from sandstone to brass, silverware, leather belts, wallets and handbags, beautiful saris and casual cotton clothing all make delightful gifts.

Gems

The gem-centre of Sri Lanka is at Ratnapura, with many of the best stones finding their way to the jewellery shops in Kandy and

One colour is applied at a time to build up a complex batik picture.

Colombo. Rubies, sapphires, cat's eyes, amethysts, zircons, alexandrites and star rubies are found in abundance and can be purchased separately as stones or set in rings and brooches. Of course, there are plenty of fakes around along with fraudsters happy to sell them to you, so take care to buy only from reputable dealers. The State Gem Corporation, 310 Galle Road, Colombo 3, will give free gem tests, but can do nothing to help you get your money back.

Masks

The extravagant, fierce-looking masks that form part of Sri Lanka's traditional dances make great ornaments. They range in size from key-ring attachments to suitcase-fillers. The craftsmen of Ambalangoda are the best mask-carvers, and you should be able to find their work in Colombo as well.

Tea

Tea from the highland plantations will refresh you long after you've left Sri Lanka. Many of the plantations have factory tours and sell packets of their own tea. Alternatively, you can buy gift packs at the Sri Lankan Tea Board, 574 Galle Road, Colombo 3, or at the airport Tea Centre.

Dining Out

Sri Lankan cuisine, while not as famous as that of its south Asian neighbours, still manages to pack a punch, and that's not just because of the incendiary strength of the curry. Rather, it's the result of two ingredients the nation possesses in abundance—fish and fruit, both flavoursome and exotic.

To Start With...

Breakfast is one of the great treats in Sri Lanka, because wherever you are staying you'll almost certainly start with a plate of delicious fresh fruit. Hotels catering for foreigners will always follow with a Western-style breakfast. But for a more adventurous start to the day try the Sri Lankan version—the hopper. Hoppers are a type of pancake made from rice flour and are, ideally, crisp on the outside and soft in the middle. The most popular are egg hoppers, fried with an egg inside, and string hoppers, where the rice-flour dough has been moulded into spaghetti-like strands. Hoppers are eaten with curry at breakfast and guaranteed to set you up for the day.

Main Courses

Several of the luxury restaurants in Colombo specialize in Chinese, Indian, Thai and Japanese menus, with a few offering Italian and even German food. The big American fast-food chains have arrived in town, proving popular with younger citizens.

Good quality Sri Lankan cuisine can be found at some of the big hotels, but for the best in traditional fare you'll have to look outside the capital. Rice and curry features heavily in the Sri Lankan diet and it's always very spicy, so proceed with caution. The curry will normally be either meat, chicken, fish or vegetable, hotted up with different combinations of the island's famous spices: coriander, turmeric, cinnamon, paprika, ground ginger, cloves and chillies. Coconut milk is also an essential ingredient. As a rule of thumb, remember that the hotness of a curry depends on the amount of chilli and ginger added. The redder the sauce, the more fire in the taste. Yellow curry contains a lot of turmeric. Black curry (a Sri Lankan speciality) puts the emphasis on cumin seeds. White curry has no chilli and is therefore the mildest.

Experts advise against drinking water with curry; instead of extinguishing the fire it exacerbates the problem. Beer or coconut milk is good, but a mouthful of cooling yoghurt or cucumber would be better by far.

Other rice dishes include *biriyani* rice, cooked in stock and served with hard-boiled eggs, meat, chicken or fish; *kool*, rice boiled and fried with vegetables; and *lamprai*, bouillon-boiled rice with dry curry, baked in a banana leaf. Floppy pancakes (*roti*) and crisp poppadoms accompany all the dishes described above. You may also be offered patties or fritters containing vegetables, meat or fish.

At every meal you will probably be presented with a little bowl of *sambol*. This fiery concoction is made of coconut, dried fish, pickles, onions, lime juice and generous quantities of chilli.

Fish

Sri Lanka is a great place for fish lovers. The mealtime stalwart is the seer, a meaty fish that's especially good cooked in lemon sauce. But there's more exotic fare: spiny lobster, tiger prawns, squid, crab and oysters are all delicious and in Sri Lanka come at affordable prices. The southern part of the island meanwhile has won local renown for its *ambul thriyal* (sour tuna-fish curry).

Desserts

After a meal of spicy curry, cool off with curd (from buffalo milk) with treacle, or *wattallapam*, baked custard. *Pani pol* is a small coconut and honey cake, while *bolo fiado*, a raisin and cashew layer cake, originated with the Portuguese colonizers. *Jaggery*, a chewy sweet, is made with crystallized palm sap.

Fruits

Sri Lanka's culinary glory is its stunning array of fruit: papayas, lychee-like rambutans, succulent mangoes, pineapples, custard apples, guavas, watermelons, passion fruit and delicious purple mangosteens, best in June. To top it all there's the amazing durian—a fruit that smells dreadful but tastes sublime.

Drinks

All manner of fresh fruit juices are available and always a treat. For a quick roadside refresher, sip coconut water straight from the *thambili* (king coconut). Toddy is an alcoholic coconut drink made from the sap of the coconut bud, while arrack, distilled from toddy, is downright potent and best consumed as a cocktail with fruit juice. Sri Lankan beer is satisfyingly flavoursome. But the classic drink is Ceylon tea which, as any Sri Lankan will tell you, is the best in the world.

Sports

Water Sports

With its superb golden beaches and sultry, sun-kissed climate, Sri Lanka is inevitably a haven for lovers of water sports. Swimmers are spoilt for choice, although they need to take care around some of the west coast resorts. Strong currents can be a danger here, so always respect the red warning flags.

Snorkelling and scuba-diving are popular pursuits off the south-west coast, due to the magnificent coral reef and its attendant tropical fish, as well as a number of shipwrecks that can be seen. Windsurfing can be enjoyed at all the main resorts, while water-skiing and sailing are especially good on the calmer waters of the Bentota River.

Fishing

Deep-sea fishing for marlin, yellowfish and shark is a thrilling experience. Trincomalee is the best-known point of departure, but being an east coast port there are the inevitable restrictions in place. On the less problematic west coast, you can take a boat out from Weligama Bay.

The large rivers flowing down from the central hills provide some excellent fresh-water fishing opportunities. You can enjoy the pleasures of trout-fishing in the tropics for the price of a licence.

Hiking

The scenic central hills provide excellent terrain for hikers. The breathtaking landscape of the Horton Plains is best appreciated on foot and there are some truly superb hikes to be had in the area, the most popular being to the dramatic World's End. For tougher uphill climbs, nothing can beat a walk to the top of Adam's Peak. It's a seven kilometre climb and rewards with spectacular views.

Golf

Sri Lanka has two first-rate golf courses which have survived intact from the British era, the Royal Colombo Golf Club and the Nuwara Eliya. Both are open to visitors, and offer very different golfing climates, one steamily tropical, the other subject to the cool winds of the mountains.

Tennis

You'll find tennis courts at many of the big hotels along the south-west coast (avoid playing in the middle of the day), as well as at the Hill Club in Nuwara Eliya.

The Hard Facts

To help you plan your trip, here are some of the practical details you should know about Sri Lanka.

Airport

All flights from abroad land at Bandaranaike International Airport, 30 km (19 miles) north of Colombo at Katunayake. There are several bank counters available for changing up money after you've passed through customs, as well as a hotel booking desk, a pre-paid taxi counter and a tourist information office.

As you leave the airport you will be bombarded by offers from taxi and hotel touts to whisk you off to Colombo. If you're not already being met by a tour operator, make sure you check the price of the taxi and/or hotel and are happy with it. Otherwise, you may want to consider using the pre-paid service. If you want to avoid taxis altogether, there are buses running from the airport to the Bastian Mawatha Bus Station in Colombo Fort.

When you're flying out, be sure to leave plenty of time for getting to the airport as security is very tight indeed. All vehicles are checked before being allowed to approach the terminal, which invariably causes delays. After checking in you will be required to pay a Rs 500 departure tax, so make sure you keep back enough to cover this. There's an extensive range of duty-free shopping available and the airport also boasts a Tea Centre. Don't hold onto rupees with the intention of using them up at the Duty Free: all transactions are in foreign currencies, with rates fixed against the US dollar.

Climate

Sri Lanka is a tropical country lying close to the equator and as such has year-round high temperatures coupled with high humidity in the lowland areas. Average monthly temperatures are around 27°C (80°F). The central hills are noticeably cooler, and the monthly average here drops to 16°C (60°F).

The country is subject to two annual monsoons. Between May and August there's a southwest monsoon, while a second one comes from the northeast in December and January. The rainfall can come in astonishingly intense bursts and roads occasionally end up like rivers. Being typically tropical, the downpours often let up as quickly as they arrive, and on most days during the monsoon months there will also be hot and sunny periods.

Communications

The postal service is generally good. The General Post Office in Janadhipathi Mawatha, Colombo Fort is open 24 hours a day, but even the smallest towns have a post office or sub-post office.

International Direct Dialling (IDD) is available at most big hotels, and increasingly from public pay phones using telephone cards. There are plenty of phone booths around Colombo, and the cards can be bought at post offices and nearby shops. Note that they are operated by different companies, such as Lanka (with yellow and blue booths) and Metrocard (with orange and black ones), whose cards are not interchangeable. If you haven't got access to IDD you can make operator-assisted international calls from the Overseas Telecommunications Service on Lower Chatham Street in Colombo Fort, which is open 24 hours, or by calling the operator, tel. 100 (or tel. 101 outside Colombo). Off-peak rates apply from 10 p.m. to 6 a.m.

Faxes can be sent from private Communications Agencies as well as the major hotels. E-mail services are available through Lanka Internet, 35 Galle Face Court 1 (info@lanka.net).

Crime

Serious or violent crime directed against foreigners is extremely rare in Sri Lanka. Petty theft is a problem, though, and you will need to take the necessary precautions. Don't leave cash and other valuables lying around in your hotel room—carry your passport, traveller's cheques, etc in a money belt or sealable pocket, or make use of the hotel safe. Be especially vigilant in crowded places where pickpockets operate, such as buses, trains and busy tourist sites.

Customs

You are allowed to bring into Sri Lanka duty free 200 cigarettes or 50 cigars or 375 g of tobacco, 1.5 litres of spirits and 2 bottles of wine and a small quantity of perfume and travel souvenirs up to $250 in value. Antiques, which in Sri Lanka mean objects more than 50 years old, cannot be taken out of the country.

Driving

Sri Lankan roads offer a prolonged white-knuckle ride that fun-fair owners could only dream of matching. Potholed and narrow, packed with lorries and buses whose drivers seem to have graduated from the madcap school of motoring, and lined with pedestrians, cyclists and animals constantly poised to launch themselves in front of oncoming traffic without so much as a glance, they are best left to the experts. For this reason, hiring a car and driver is a sensible option for getting around the country, often cheaper and certainly less stressful than renting a self-drive car. There are many agencies offering good deals that include petrol and the driver's subsistence (you might be able to negotiate unlimited mileage as well), and there's the bonus that most drivers are also very knowledgeable guides.

If you do decide to go it alone, remember that traffic keeps to the left in Sri Lanka. Speed limits are 56 kph (35 mph) in towns and built-up areas and 72 kph (45 mph) elsewhere. Beware of oncoming overtaking vehicles especially on bends, and try not to drive at night when conditions become even more hazardous.

Emergencies

For emergency services in Colombo dial: police, 433333; ambulance/fire, 422222. There's also a Tourist Police Division, tel. 432635. Outside the city, ask at your hotel reception or the local police station.

Embassies are located in Colombo. They should be contacted only for serious situations such as a lost passport or worse, and not for lost plane tickets or money.

Formalities

Tourists from more that 60 countries are not required to obtain visas prior to visiting Sri Lanka. Nationals of the United States, Australia and New Zealand receive a 90-day tourist visa on entry, while those from the United Kingdom, Canada, France and Germany receive 30-day visas. It's fairly easy to get extensions if necessary. Make sure, however, that your passport is valid for at least three months before its expiry date.

Health

Before you leave, be sure to buy travel insurance that includes medical cover and have all the necessary immunizations—contact your doctor or travel centre to find out what's required. You'll also need to start taking a course of antimalarial tablets a few days prior to departure. It's a good idea to take mosquito repellent cream as well.

With a little care, you should encounter no health problems during your stay. It's wise to avoid too much exposure to the sun. Remember, you are almost on the equator and the sun is 59 extremely powerful here. Wear a hat, use a good sun-screen and keep in the shade as much as possible, especially in the middle of the day.

Drink plenty of mineral water to avoid dehydration—but never drink tap water. In the same vein, try to avoid salad and fruit that's been washed in unpurified water.

Holidays and festivals

There are several religious festivals that are observed as holidays, many of which are based on the lunar calendar and therefore not on fixed dates. Each full moon is *poya* day, a Buddhist holy day when shops and offices shut. The Muslim community observe Ramadan, Id-ul-Azha, Id-ul-Fitr and Milad-un-Nabi (Mohammed's birthday). Ask at the Tourist Office for the specific dates when you arrive. Other public holidays in Sri Lanka are:

January	Thai Pongal (Hindu)
February 4	National Day
February/March	Maha Sivarathri (Hindu)
March/April	Good Friday
April 13/14	Sinhalese and Tamil New Year
May 1	May Day
May 22	National Heroes' Day
June 30	Bank Holiday
October	Deepavali (Hindu)
December 25	Christmas Day
December 31	New Year Bank Holiday

Languages

The two national languages are Sinhala and Tamil. English is widely spoken and will steer you through most encounters with Sri Lankans, although this may not be the case if you head out to the more remote villages. If you want to surprise people by greeting them in their own language, here are a few key phrases in Sinhala:

Ayubowan	May you live long (standard greeting)
Ou/Naa	Yes/No
Honday	OK
Kohomadha?	How are you?
Bohoma rahai!	That was delicious!

and a couple of words in Tamil:

Vanakkam	Hello
Aamaa/Illa	Yes/No

Media

Sri Lanka has an excellent range of English-language newspapers and magazines. *The Daily News*, the *Evening Observer* and *The Island* are all printed daily. *The Island* also has a Sunday edition, which competes with the *Sunday Times*, *Sunday Observer* and *Sunday Leader*. The *Midweek Mirror* comes out each Wednesday, while the *Lanka Guardian* is an informative current-affairs magazine that appears every two weeks.

The Sri Lanka Broadcasting Corporation's Radio Sri Lanka channel has regular national and international news and takes in programmes from the BBC. There are plenty of upbeat English-language FM radio stations, such as Yes, Sun and Capital Radio, which concentrate on pop music.

The government-run television stations, Rupavahini 1 and 2 and ITN have programmes in English as well as Sinhalese and Tamil. Other stations with English programmes include MTV, which has an intake from BBC World News, Dynavision, which does the same with CNN, Swarnavahini and Sirasa TV.

With a short-wave radio, you can listen to the BBC World Service or Voice of America. It's best to find out the frequencies on which they broadcast before you leave as they change at different times of the day.

Money
The unit of currency in Sri Lanka is the *rupee* (Rs or Re), which is divided into 100 *cents* (c). Coins: 5, 10, 25 and 50 cents, and Rs 1, 2, 5 and 10. Notes: Rs 10, 20, 50, 100, 200, 500 and 1,000. Shopkeepers and traders are often reluctant to accept large denomination notes, so be sure to break them into smaller amounts whenever possible.

Traveller's cheques can easily be changed at banks. Another way to obtain cash is with a bank card, using your regular PIN code. At the moment this service is available only with Visa cards via the cash dispensers (ATMs) at the Colombo and Kandy branches of the Hong Kong and Shanghai Bank. Major international credit cards are widely accepted in the larger hotels, shops and restaurants.

The Sri Lankan rupee is not a convertible currency, which means that you won't be able to change it after you've left the country. The main banks have offices at the airport where you can reconvert rupees into foreign currency before you fly out, but make sure you've kept any bank or ATM receipts as you may have to show them.

Opening hours
We give the following times as a general guide, some of them subject to variations.

Government offices open Monday to Friday 9 a.m.–5 p.m.

Banks open Monday to Friday 9 a.m.–1 p.m. or 3 p.m.

Post office hours are Monday to Friday 8.30 a.m.–5 p.m., Saturdays 8.30 a.m.–1 p.m.

Most shops are open Monday to Friday 8.30 or 9 a.m.–7 p.m. and on Saturdays until 3 p.m.

Note: *Poya* days (each full moon) are holidays and shops and offices may be closed.

Photography

When taking photographs, bear in mind that for most of the day the sunlight in Sri Lanka is extremely powerful, and exposure needs to be adjusted accordingly. Be sure to store film in a cool, dry place. It's best to take sufficient rolls of film with you. If you should need to buy any while you're there, only go to a reputable outlet and always check the expiry date.

Permits are required for photographing the ancient sites at Sigiriya, Polonnaruwa and Anuradhapura, obtainable from the relevant archaeological museums. These are still important religious sites: never photograph someone or have yourself photographed in front of a temple statue or painting. Ask permission before taking a person's picture. And don't even think about photographing military installations, army and police checkpoints, the Port Authority area in Colombo and other sensitive security hotspots.

Public Transport

Trains. Sri Lanka's trains amble along at a sedate pace, but are probably the most comfortable way to travel around the country. There are only a few main lines, but they reach all the major tourist destinations and at a remarkably low price. First-class carriages are generally very comfortable and some are air-conditioned. Second class has soft seats and is normally calmer than third class, which can be something of a scrum.

The hub of the network is Colombo's Fort Station, from where all trains depart. The line east to Kandy and Matale is especially scenic, and you can travel in a first-class "observation saloon" to enjoy the best views. The Colombo-Matara line, which goes via the coastal resorts and Galle, has only second- and third-class carriages. There's also a northern line up to Anuradhapura and across to Trincomalee.

Special tourist trains are often put on and provide a more luxurious style of travel. For information, ask at the Tourist Office or call Fort Station, tel. 435838.

Buses. You will find two principal types of bus. The rickety, yellow CTB buses operate along local and long-distance routes. They are cheaper but slower than the inter-city private buses, which are often newer vehicles boasting air-conditioning. These are undoubtedly the fastest things on the road.

Taxis. Ideally, taxis should be metered. In practice, you'll probably need to agree on a price before you get in. Radio cab firms, such as GNTC (tel. 688688) or Kangaroo Cabs (tel. 502888), offer a more upmarket service, with standard rates, digital meters and air-conditioning.

Three-wheelers. Noisy little auto-rickshaws buzz around Sri Lankan towns like flies. They're very nippy among heavy traffic and there's never any trouble in finding one (they'll keep bothering you, in fact), but be certain to fix the price before you climb in.

Social customs

Sri Lankans are an easy-going people, but they also hold to certain codes of behaviour which all visitors should respect. When entering a temple or shrine, shoes must be removed and heads uncovered; shorts, short skirts and singlets are inappropriate. At the beach, nudity and topless bathing are forbidden.

Time

Sri Lanka is 5$\frac{1}{2}$ hours ahead of GMT. It has recently introduced daylight-saving in summer, when it becomes GMT+6.

Tipping

A 10% service charge will automatically be added onto the bill at hotels and restaurants, so everything will cost a little more than you expect, and any additional rounding up is entirely at your discretion. It's customary to tip porters (about Rs 10 per bag), taxi drivers and hotel maids.

Toilets

Public toilets are few and far between in Sri Lanka, and then will generally be of the "squat" rather than sit-down variety. If this is a problem, take advantage of the facilities at a tourist-friendly hotel or restaurant.

Tourist Information Offices

The Ceylon Tourist Board has its headquarters at 78, Steuart Place, Galle Road, Colombo 3; tel. 437059/437060; fax 437953. There are also offices at Bandaranaike International Airport and Kandy (see inside back cover).

The Tourist Board can help with accommodation and general information on where and how to travel around the country. They also publish two free magazines each month, *Travel Lanka* and *Explore Sri Lanka*.

Voltage

Electric current is 230–240V, 50 cycles AC. Sockets take three-pronged plugs. If you are planning to take sensitive electrical equipment, such as a laptop computer, it's probably a good idea to use a voltage stabilizer.

INDEX

Adam's Peak 34–35
Ambalangoda 23
Anuradhapura 37–41
Aukana 41
Bentota 22–23
Beruwala 22–23
Colombo 13–19
  Cinnamon Gardens 16
  Fort 14–16
  Galle Face Green 16–18
  Pettah 15–16
Dambulla 47
Dehiwala Zoo 18–19
Dondra Head 26
Ella 35
Galle 24–26
Gal Vihara 45
Hakgala Botanical Garden 34
Hambantota 27
Hikkaduwa 23
Horton Plains 35
Kalutara 22
Kandy 29–33
Kataragama 27
Kelaniya Raja Maha Vihara 19

Matara 26
Mihintale 41
Mount Lavinia 19
Mount Pidurutalagala 33
Negombo 21–22
Nilaveli 49
Nuwara Eliya 33–34
Peradeniya Botanic Gardens 31
Pinnawela Elephant Orphanage 33
Polonnaruwa 41–47
Ratnapura 34
Sigiriya 46
Tangalla 27
Tea Plantations 33–34
Temple of the Tooth 29–30
Trincomalee 48–49
Unawatuna 26
Uppuveli 49
Weligama 26
World's End 35
Yala National Park 27

GENERAL EDITOR:
  Barbara Ender-Jones
EDITOR:
  Christina Grisewood
LAYOUT:
  Luc Malherbe
PHOTO CREDITS:
  Volkmar E. Janicke:
    front cover; pp. 32, 44
  Bernard Joliat:
    back cover, pp. 6, 12, 19, 53
  Hémisphères/Sassi: p. 1
  Hémisphères/Colin:
    pp. 2, 5, 17, 25, 47
  Hémisphères/Frances:
    pp. 20, 28, 36, 40
MAPS:
  Elsner & Schichor
  JPM Publications

Copyright © 2000
by JPM Publications S.A.
12, avenue William-Fraisse,
1006 Lausanne, Switzerland
E-mail:
information@jpmguides.com
Web site:
http://www.jpmguides.com/

Printed in Switzerland
Gessler/Sion (CTF)